Colors of Life

Hansika Parmar

**First Edition Published in 2021 by
Brown Page Publication**
29(a) Faizupur Khadar Tigaon 90
Ballabgarh Faridabad Haryana 121101
Contact: +91-7428778978

ISBN: "978-81-952388-0-4"

Acknowledgement

I'd like to thank my parents for their support and my sister for her enthusiasm towards my work. I'd like to thank my publishing team for their work behind the final result. I'd also like to express my gratitude towards Mr. Piyush Arora for his patience while working with me.

And I'd love to thank all the people who are indirectly a part of inspiration towards the working of my book.

Thank you.

About the Author.

Hansika Parmar

Hansika Parmar is a student, born and brought up on the Land of the Rajputs,

She is a graduate of Hospitality and Hotel Administration from Institute of Hotel Management, Ahmedabad. She is currently working in Dubai. She is a beginner in writing and looking forward to new experiences. According to her, writing provides her patience and calms her soul. She has a cheerful soul and a kind heart. Her writings are inspired by nature, reality of life and love at first sight. She is a believer.

This book contains poems from some common genre. The classification is done to have an easier understanding of the same.

WRITER ME

A writer has the most emotionally active mind, and while it is working it creates one of the best words that can be possible. Some of the same words and phrases are settled up below. Feel what your mind says and love what your heart says. Write to get better and write to feel worse.

WRITE AGAIN

Sitting in the crowd
Still not have a sound
Walking all about
The day had spent aloud

My head screams all in pain
My words all go in vain
That's the time to grab a pen
And start to write again

My abstracts all there in words
My pain is on the unknown furs
The world is hidden all up my brain
And i started to write again

Someday I'll pray alive
To prove that words are lie
Everyday would live again
When i start to write again

LOVE

Falling in love is one of the best feelings which doesn't take much time to go the other way. Here I have tried to cover all aspects of love in mere words to express what I have been feeling and have felt in my life. Love is theonly thing that doesnt ask for your race, religion, age and sex. I hope it stays the same forever.

FOR THE FIRST TIME

When we met for the first time
The clock did stop
My body shivered in order
To absorb your warmth

We stood far away
But my eyes got stuck on you
How can i not enjoy
A beautiful view like you

Just walk a little slowly
Across the crowd
Clearing all the distances
And all the doubts

You came in front of me
Just to get a good stare
I came to see what do they say
About the love in my first glare.

LOVE

I stood on the edge thinking to take the step dead
He pushed and pulled me back at the same time ahead
My heart skipped a beat
He said, " That's how it feels. "
I came back steps and saw in his eyes
The fear of losing all that lies
I said, " It's not like that"
I just came here to see the brightness set
His face said OHH LIAR.
But all that his lips said was, "What happened babe?"
And all I said was every tear I felt.

I'M LUCKY

I If we think about that night
A lot could've changed
So that we won't be what we are
Or what we're gonna be

If we think about that night
A lot could have changed
You could've been busy somewhere else
Or i could've been thinking something else

We could've not be getting that feeling
Or we could've done what we thought
We could've hide that words inside
Or we could've not shared secrets at night

There could've been a lot of changes
If things didn't happen in our lives as they did
I'm glad that it happened as it is
I'm lucky that I got to love you.

I`LL BE WITH YOU ❤

I'll be there when the sun sets
I'll be there when the ocean melts
I'll be there when the pain is at peak
Like the itch that can never reek

I'll stand when they all leave
I'll sit when you're asleep
I'll walk when you're tired
I'll stop when you're admired

I'll keep all the memories
I'll write all the stories
I'll cook the meals together
I'll sleep when you're forever

I'll be night to make you shine
I'll be the sun to give you light
I'll be the green to let you breathe
I'll be the dream to make you smile

THE DATE

Met at a casual talk as colleagues
Later came upto names
He called her on her phone
And she called him by his name

They had something they didn't realise
An understanding of two old flies
They shared their thoughts and realised
They not just friends they're butterflies

They went out twice don't call it a date
Just casual outing with a break
They talked all night and thought it good
They didn't know what it could become

One day he asked her out on movie
She said who else is there
He shrugged a little with a smile so clear
And replied let's call it a date dear.

FIRST LOVE

At first you don't realize its true
You found the love you wanted to
Then how are you gonna tell him that
As he doesn't know that's what he felt

She saw him talking across the room
And caved her hair behind her ear
He saw her and took off his eyes
But what to do of these butterflies

They started talking as the event came by
Became friends before they got else to say
He asked her what is in your heart
Don't say like you don't know the art

They spend the month all good and best
Later faced the heart that had to melt
It wasn't a thing that had happened before
It wasn't a feeling that they could now adore.

HIS THOUGHTS ABOUT HER

Her eyes are like pearls to him and her hair like the ocean waves. There are a thousand lines which are enough to describe his love for her. Some of the same lines are here below trying to enhance what one feels about his lover.

HER

I saw her walking away
Like an ice from fire
Tired of melting enough
Scared of losing her identity

She knew i can't live without her
She knew I'd rather die
Still she had to leave
Making all those lies

I waited for hours
I waited for days
Just saw her shadow moving away
To a world unknown to me

What did i do, i don't know
What can i do, i don't know
What should i do, I'll never know
What would time do, I'll come to know

I woke up suddenly
Maintaining heavy breaths
Saw her head on my chest
My heart just came back to life

Kept on gazing her the rest of the night
Realised that love is blind
And I'm blindly in love
With just the sleep of hers beside me

THE RED DRESS

There she is
Standing in the red dress
With her shoes in her hand
Having a gaze at my face

Looking as good as i can
In a sober dress as tux
May it be a three piece or two
Feeling light like water

Her blush was more real
Than the roses born today
My eyes which can't get off her
Had that effect i guess

Holding my hand
She looked in my eyes
And said, "Hi handsome"
Should I say something?

Well i had to
"Ummmm... Yeah"
Her smile grew
I held her face in my palm

Our eyes met
Her lips red
I kissed her all the way
She realised what i couldn't say

That she is my breath
That only she can take away

WATER

I swim in the ocean for hours
To find the perfect waves
To get the perfect space
And to make it ripple in ways

Ended up in her house
Like an ocean cave
In the middle of the water
Like the beauty of the waves

Touch her and she rolls away
Like the fish in your tank
She's the love of the blue
Like the corals pushed to reef

The blue of the ocean
Took its colour from her eyes
The waves from the hair
And the life from her smile

She's the grace of god
Placed upon the world
She's the water in the ocean
That makes the death reverse

BE HERE

Turned around to see his eyes
Filled with cries and tears
Not letting me go away
From his arms around my tires

Spend all my life with him
But can't refuse the time
Has love ever been so cruel
As i am acting tonight

Fell hard on his chest
Crunched all bones at my best
Tears are not just his right
I'll be here after it all right

HER THOUGHTS ABOUT HIM

It is always said that girls feel superior to boys as compared to boys, well I don't know the truth hidden but I have tried to get that feeling into words of my own. What that says is just a reflection of what they are not able to say and what they feel is always a secret. I hope you get to hear their feelings when you need to.

THAT SUIT

I saw him enter
In that navy blue suit
His walk was like the winter
That tied my eyes in it

The room was filled with humour
And some old fake stories
I hope when we talk here
You share what is real

It's not just that the suit
Took all of my soul
It's just that he looks so stunning
My heart cant get away too soon

Fly me to the moon
With these shoulders and that height
I won't mind being your today
And hope you won't leave tonight

I'm still on other side of the room
And i know you've just entered
But what to do of my sight
That dreams about you in that suit.

I walked around the sight of yours
To get stuck in the gaze of those eyes
You knew what you're going through
You knew what we could become
You knew what i was doing

Still you didn't turn back to see
The dress i wore in such a glee

Is it like you to turn away
From girls that ask you to stay
Or is it just me standing here
To embarrass you at this atmosphere
I hope we meet again someday
When the stars are the only one that see
The spark so bright that shines so high
That the future comes right to our eyes.

AFTER THAT NIGHT

On a sunny day
Wanting for you to stay
Here in this room
Alone and abloom

Filled with the horror
Of our stay over
Thinking of the word
To start it all over

Should I say hi !!
Would it sound goodbye
Or wait for him
To say something

That finishes my wait
To hear him say a name
Which creates a smile
To my lips for a while

But there he is
Changing the course
Of my flowing thoughts
And not even saying adieu.

A BOY

I saw all the stories
I sang all the songs
I dreamt her being pretty
And i saw him being strong

I saw what she was
And what she was gonna become
I saw him in a shadow black
And her being the white so pure

But i don't get this point
Why only bad guys get what they want
What about the girls in black
Can't someone cut them some slack

Get them a guy with the cutest of smile
The one who's known to be purest of white
A guys who makes her perfectly smile
A boy who calls her "perfectly mine"

.

FEEL

I don't know if I can make your heart to change
So I'll write a better song to make it rain
I can see the light that you try to make it hide
They tell me that you have had a lot to fight
I hope this just makes you feel alive
I hope this just makes you feel tonight

I saw you there in the park with all alone
I came by to see if you can see me go
But your mind was somewhere else aside
Someplace where i didn't seem to walk in light
So i just hope this makes you feel alive
I just hope this makes you feel tonight

I'll be there when the day seems to be gone
And the night is crawling up along its own
And you see me with the spark inside
And we can have some time tonight
So i just hope this makes you feel alive
And I just hope this makes you feel tonight.

<u>FRIENDSHIP</u>

There is nothing better to describe life than happiness. People give away their lives and kill for it. If you have somebody with whom you can share anything and everything is your friend. All that you need to get through your life is someone to share it with.

COLLEGE DAYS

I entered in the place
To witness my own space
Left all the love at home
Which was far away alone

Got hostel with two roomies
Were not that shy but bloomies
We started sharing words
Then ended sharing lives

Had classes everyday
Of studies and of plays
Faced all the new of phases
With a group of new faces

Seven of us alone
Were enough to be a bone
We saw all the dark sides
And witnessed the real lives

We used to talk about
All the useless crowd
What we didn't even know
That these hearts would have to go

We saw each other last
One year ago in past
We're gonna go out and plan
To create those days again

GOA

The sound of the water
Made the breeze run away
You saw what all happened
And still chose to stay

Had a whole lot of beer
And some lot of wine
Slept all that long days
But remember all nights

See the Ocean and Sun
Talk to each one and none
Feel the softest of sounds
Of the Ocean and crowds

Got your hair braided long
Sing loudest of songs
You're lucky of bonds
To go to Goa all along

EMBRACE HER FEMININITY

What she can do is everything and what she can't do is nothing. All that she needs is the will power to prove her worth to herself. She's the reason of existence and she is the one who plays all the roles possible

THE DAUGHTER

Holding dad's hand when to walk
Doing mistakes after every pep talk
Eating food from mum's hand daily
Scolding younger sibling willingly
Dancing around the house without a reason
Nothing i do would be considered treason
Getting a chocolate for every good deed
And all sitting together to eat
I wish my little life was not all messy
I wish a daughter's life was that easy

SHE

She is a strand of brave
And a bunch of shy
She is as soft as a kiss
And as rude as sky
She is the queen of happy
And the kid of cry
But she's the reason
Of smile when one passes by

She's the blood of alive
And the breath of dead
She's the reality of life
And the virtuality of lie
She's the tear of your eyes
And the teeth of your smile
But she's the reason
Of your smile when you're alive

She has a heart of gold
And a dress of pray
She has a crown and
And a doll to help her play
She's the girl of your dreams
And the cause of your fear
She's the one you can hold
When you want someone dear

DAUGHTER OF THE WAR

She floats like a dream,
Before she sinks under,
Carrying in her folds,
The dying cries of the soldiers...

The sorrow of their widows
And the deaths of their lovers
The emptiness that lies
In the grounds of their coven

She has the power of their hearts
Which gives her voice the strength
To fulfil her life with no regrets
And live her life with full health

She saw every bit too early
Young mind which saw the war
Young heart which cried everyday
To the death of those she abhor

She has got the guts to fight alone
And the mind to beat them all
She is the daughter of the war
And the sister of them all.

MIRROR

Her eyes like two stars gazing me
Her blush like the rose everyone craves for
Her lips like the cool breeze after a stormy night
Her hair like the waves of the ocean calling me
Her smile, ohh it's just the moon nothing else
Her face like the light of the sun
Her presence a happy day
Her soul my divine desire
She's the reason i fall for myself
Coz when you look in the mirror she's right there

YOUR EYES

When i see it in the mirror
I see the big brown eyes
Which hold all the stars
And hide all the big great lies

They've seen the childhood small
And made the waterfall
They've closed when all alone
And opened up to you when none

There balls are not just eyes
They're the memories alive
They tell you the déjà vus
And create new ones to prove

Just see through them one day
They'll tell you what they say
They'll show you who's not real
And hid all of your fears

LEAL

She can't be called as a liar
Even when her thoughts are on fire
She is the pillar of truth
And has the base of the ground

She can be called a sapphire
As her skin is so pure
She smiled and the world
Just gave it all away

She can be called as the morning
As her eyes are so sure
They give the light to the tired
And the brightness to the day

She can be called to be leal
As her thoughts are so real
Her trust is like the mountain
That only she can maintain

<u>FAMILY</u>

Families are history and their future is a mystery. All that you need for support is called a family. They will be there always and forever.

THE GIFT

The girl said her gift is the best
She got a necklace and a set
Bought too much expensive shoes
Attractive ways to drink her booze

The boy said his gift was the best
He got a car that passed the test
Bought a watch which got the show
Said he's the most expensive boo

The kid got his gift that looked so good
Showed his phone with recent hood
Hugged his mum and dad so tight
They made his day with best of light

The best gift if you ask from me
Would be a child to his mummy
His small hands which held her so tight
And saw her face with first of sight

MOTHER❤

She's got the grace
Of a fallen angel
She's got the smile
Like a cloud's silver line
She's got the love
More than anyone above
She has the magic
All the world combined
She's not yours
She's mine
Her care has the power
To heal all wounds
She's not just my lover
She's my mother

PARENTS

You see them move
You hold their groove
You climb them up
You push them down

You shout their names
You call their blames
You hide what's right
They tell you're bright

Their love isn't a lie
You can't imagine why
You can never gain your talents
Without the love of your parents

THE GHOST...

He walked through that door
In a vest and alone
Gave a smile around the room
Just to hide all his mourn

He saw the lady cry in black
Tried to tell her that he's back
Ran even shouting close to her
Watched her saying all those words

He rushed in to hug her tight
His hands just came through her life
Realised he's not alive
Realised his life's a lie

Watched around to see them mourn
Stopped at his daughter who seem to smile
His legs slowly walked to her
She said, " Now you're my Angel"

<u>NATURE</u>

My inspiration and my enthusiasm. My work always has an element of nature and it feels complete with it. It has been there since the beginning and will be there when we are not.

THE SUNSHINE

The sunrise paved its way
To a glory filled in day
The reality all came through
With a story of those two

They waited for the sun
To come into the light
They cried until it's done
The light was that much bright

Walking to each other
In a black and white forever
The theme was so damn sunny
That the sky was looking funny

They stared the sun to come upside
And watch them come together
The sun too took its time and came
And blessed them with sunshine.

FIRE

I am the flame
Born to bring your phoenix back to life
I'm the Ash
Where you'll come after your end
I'm the burn
On your skin when the sun stares you
I'm the blast
Of you car caused after you crashed
I can make you live
Or force you to die
I'm the protector of hell
And the purifier of lives
I'm not just a god
I'm the fire alive

CALL THE RAIN

Have you ever felt like flying
When the stormy winds cross your hair
Pushing you towards your happiness
Making you think of being a bird fair

The lightning showing their true colors
The droplets washing off your sins
The smell of earth make you feel in heaven
The voice of clouds bring you back to realm

Call the rain to make you smile
Feel the eco of the noisy drops
Deal with the water running like your blood
Reveal the truth of life with love

The talk of wind telling you the scary stories
The waves of trees telling you hope of life
The smile on faces making life far better
The spark of light making your eyes to shine

ANOTHER WORLD

Let's have a world so bright
With the story of a sun
The length of its rays
And the voice of its run

The life of a revolution
And the sorrow of a rotation
The words of a bird
And the love of a swan

The plot of a kind
With heart and a mind
The green of the trees
And the blue of the seas

What doesn't happen
When we ask for reality
The lies come true
And the false gets true.

WHEN THE SKY TALKS

I went upstairs to look the sky
When there is not much of day
I went upstairs to sing so light
The bright star shines again

I saw that wind comb through my hair
And watched it talk to me
Through narrows whooshes of sweetheart songs
And pushed me there again

I remembered us unbroken love
Talks all so smooth so brave
We kept it low for so much long
Now there's not much to say

This night brought light into my mind
I sang and cried again
If time comes soon we see the noon
I hope you're still not there

ABOUT YOURSELF

Self love and self admiration makes a person worth caring for and make sure you always have a lot of it. Keep loving yourself and be there for yourself. Then the rest of the world doesn't matter.

YOUR MIND

Is it wrong to be right
Just to let go of a fight
I know I've been wrong
I know I've hurted lives
But what if i think i was right
And was not told it's alright
Maybe you're wrong and the world is right
But that can never change your mind

Have u ever done something
That you wanted to do
But the world wouldn't understand the truth
The sky agreed you're right
The night gave a flight
To your emotions altogether
Made u underestimate your latter
Maybe you're wrong and the world is right
But that can never change your mind

Your life can be a lie
Your death will affect a fly
But who cares when I'm dead myself
Underneath my soul found its peace
In the deeds that made it alive
The world is a heaven
And maybe you're just a pawn
To show and act like a clown
Keep smiling like the clouds try
To give you rain frequently passing by
Maybe you'll find your way

And make the world change
Maybe you're wrong and the world is right
But that can never change your mind

CHOICES

Made a choice of life over death
Made a life of smiles over breath
Took a stone and stopped it from
Flying away and shattering my window
The window which i would rather open away
Let the breeze fall in
Let the life crawl in
See what the world has for me
See what my mére left for me
Took a choice of tears over joy
Saw all lives getting all back ahoy
Seen the death
Seen the life
All that made me relieve
Made all the choices that i made
Made all the choices that I made.

A NEW DAY

A step to take
For another man's sake
A life to lose
A point to choose
A selfless deed
An ego less creed
An option of life
To make me alive
For tomorrow's to decide
And live a great life
Just make a new change
Just live a new day

Create what was lost
And mend all at cost
Remember your fails
Collection of tales
Your heart has the power
And your soul's got the spark
To create a new sun
And give light to burn
You see what you made
At a scene of the wade
You made a life gay
You made a new day.

YOU ARE DONE

Life is made of
A thousand little stories
And it has made us do
A thousand little crimes

What made you change
Your mind about living
Is it the noise created
By the back door or behind

Ever faced these dark doors
Ever messed with darker minds
Ever had a look at ones face
And thought if they aren't kind

Ever kicked someone's food
Or broke their heart about
The talks of weary eyes
And bodies that have no doubt

Ever cursed one to die alone
And feared what you've done
Ever made a choice in life
That made you think you're done

LONELY ASS DRIVE

.

Sat under the stars with the sand on my toes
Watched the water run by like a wind in the sky
Met all new of lives everyday in my time
I scorned all of my smiles for some lonely ass drive.

Ate food of all kinds with sauces and limes
Drank whole lot of wine with shaking ass guys
Danced in every old bar with DJs and guitars
Scorned all of my smiles for a lonely ass drive

They told me to stay but i had to leave
Find my own little peace and be away from these
So i took my stuff and kissed goodbye to mom
She said I scorned all of my smiles for a lonely ass drive.

<u>HEARTBREAK</u>

Everything that breaks a heart doesn't deserve to be happy. Pain is the answer to it and loneliness is the afterlife. So take care and live your life to the fullest.

PAIN

For everyone pain is different
For her pain is love
The hurt can never be measured above
For him pain is heartbreak
Which can't be explained
For her pain is words
The speech of cowards
For him pain is quiet
The death can only decide
For her pain is noise
When one has no other choice
For him pain is sleep
Nightmares can be so deep
For her pain is glass
The piece stuck had a class
For him pain is choice
The answers can never rejoice
For her pain is tears
Best way to kick one's fears
For him pain is smile
On the face of upset minds
For her pain is death
Of someone that she does regret
For him pain is cries
Of souls leaving the body of alives
For her pain is her period
Can't be explained to be more serious
For him pain is lies
He can't see his trust die

Each heart has another pain
Each life has something to gain

<u>MUSIC</u>

My love, my life and my companion. The thing that has been there for me from the beginning. It is the only thing that has a beat that makes others live. And i hope you live your life at the fullest

MUSIC

I held its hand
And forgot the world
My life's been a hell
It seems like the rope to heaven
With it the world seems quiet
And the pain fades away
Have you ever felt the same
Like flying between the clouds
With just the waves coming
Off the earphones and its sound
May the music be your choice
May the pitch be your height
May the words be your redemption
May the bass be your anger
May the song be your life.

__DARK SIDE__

Things and situations make you a different person and bring out your dark side. The poems below have tried to describe this situation to the fullest and tried to express the same feeling.

SLEEPLESS NIGHTS

Sleepless nights with lots of sights
Incredible shadows with no lights
The sound of the little one's cries
And the feeling after my lullabies

Just scared dream away
To a place where they stay
Eating my honest smile
In a big bowl of bile

The dreams which feel true
And the shadows of the crew
The Devil's personal hour
To scare me too far

A shout at the night
Which stays till daylight
My sleeplessness lies
Under the night skies.

THE DARK NIGHT

Dark is the night,
Darker the soul,
Fathomless depths,
Stories untold...
Hearts are brave,
Walking in dark,
Stranded in fear,
Bodies apart...
Scared of the night,
Just stay in the light,
Hold something tight,
Or I will be right...
Beware of shadows,
That possess new lives,
Save your each soul,
And I hope it's not the end.

SHADOW

I've got a stalker of my own
Walking hidden in the dark
The one who's scared of the dawn
Coz the light could show it's dark

I've got a lier of my own
Who says I'll be there forever
The world can see it when it's there
Walking alongside me here

It's not that scary as it seems
It's just the dark reality
Which shows the darkened mind
Of me moving towards light

It's the silent stalker
Which scares the hell of heart
It's the same dark shadow
That rises in the dark

THE MISTAKE

I did a mistake
Coz the world believes it
I made a mother cry
Coz she releaves in me
I made a lover cry
Coz he's in love with me
I made the heaven cry
Coz it isn't gonna get me

I did a mistake
Coz the sky believes it
I couldn't stop the shower
Of water through its clouds
I wouldn't stop until
I get what i need and want
I shouldn't mind the world
Coz my peers will always be around

I did a mistake
But i don't believe it
Coz i don't have my peace until
I don't make it easy to live with me
Coz i don't need a word
Of the money minded herb which sits inside me
Coz i didn't do a mistake
I just did what I had to.

HEARTLESS

They call me heartless
When they don't know where I've been
Where I've given it away
And cried all over

Call my peers they'll say
She's everything but that
I've been called kind
My nature of living that

They call me heartless
When they couldn't see
17 hearts under my bed
Ready to be crushed by just a word

A word that has the power to break it
An emotion which doesn't make me care
The lives of people surrounding me
Makes me live a life without it

A life without the heart of mine
I·don't know where it's kept
Or broken and thrown into pieces
Hidden into places no one could reach

Peaches are the life of those who have the life with their
hearts placed
Don't worry my love I've been this way for a long time
I've been Heartless.

DISAPPEAR

You are pretty
Like the red roses
You are made to shine
Like the bright stars

You're the yellow
Of the daffodils
And the thing that
Won't let me move on

When i think of
The past experience
I get to realise
What we were

There's no one that
Knows my fears
There's no one to
To hold my tears

We've been like this
For much a year
But the love
The love never disappears
But the love never disappears

JOKER FACE

He was inside with his eyes closed
Scared to face the work disclosed
His face was painted with white n red
His lips were covered with whole regret
He looked at his red dumpling nose
Watching that his feelings arose
He missed his life that looked like him
All happy and all the smiles again
He couldn't cry if wanted to
Or else his paint would drain adieu
He stepped out of his space
Watched the world for his await
He said his sins are for a day
That wasn't at all today

<u>OTHERS</u>

Now comes a random collection of my work which carries multiple agendas and stories if you're able to decode it.

ALL COLORS

I thought i was black
A shade to be sacked
My life was brown
More of like a clown
Saw the world blue
Coz the only thing constant was the dew
Saw the people red
Their hands covered in blood
Girls are pink
As the colour shrinks
Nature is green
Everything seems so clean
But the smile of a child is white
The peace to every sight
Saw all the colours in my life
Waiting to get them all right

WHAT IF...

What if, it was all a lie
What if, you were never mine
What if, the stars were not right
What if, you weren't the daylight
What if, i fall in love
What if, it's never enough
What if, i messed it up
What if, the measurement was not a cup
What if, the glass shattered
What if, it never mattered
What if, your heart fell wrong
What if, there was no song
What if, we all can't handle
What if, it feels like we're stranded
What if, the sky isn't real
What if, the sea isn't clear
What if, i wrote all wrong
What if, i thought i'm strong
What if, i die alone
What if, i have a heart of stone
What if, i think too much
What if, i dreamt too much

AMNESIA

It would be better of i had it
I would've forgotten the pain
The lies told to you by me
The truth held by me here

It would be better if i
Hadn't been the way i was
Hadn't lived the way i did
Like the ghost of a living

It would've been easier
To live a lie
Or to live a disease
Just to be in peace

Life would've been pretty
Easier to die without pain
Nothing to lose or gain
Trying to forget my mains

It would've been easier if i had it
It would've been better if it was Amnesia

MOIRA

You got yours
I've got mine
It's like the fears
It's like the smiles

You've got the deeds
That make you shine
I've got my rumours
That are mostly lies

You can blame the fate
And just cry on your luck
Or you can realise it's not that
Which makes your buck

You do things
which makes you right
You make mistakes
Which change your lives

You meet by destiny
You meet by fate
It's what's your Moira
It's what that stays

OCCULT

I was the white
Pure and light
Your love made magic
Held me tight

Your eyes are the sky
Makes me think I'm dreaming
Your words are the stars
Shining in your eyes

There's the magic around you
Like a shield protecting
The beauty of yours
From the occult world

Stay hidden from the world love
Just meet me on Saturdays
To make my dreams shine
For better Sundays

PLAYS AND SCRIPTS

Why everytime when i look at all the lies
I see the fame of lives hidden in smiles
He says he loves me more
And wishes to say mi amor
But doesn't even realise
That it's all about what we decide

There have been few more days
Since we had our last best plays
We hid behind the glass
To hide all the fake arse
Expecting its not ajar
But what if it's out with a heavy bar

The life is not a play
To perform on a dull spent day
The world looks for the part
Which takes them out afar
They want their pain to hide
In scripts and farther strides

HOPE

What's hope
They'd say...
It's a journey
My way
Is it real?
They quere
That's faith
Oh yes!!!
They thought
I brought
My words
So light
Their faith
Did ignite
They smiled
And applied
My notion
So bright
We ended
The same
Just they added
Hopes in their name

GRAMARY

I was sitting alone in dark
Waiting for years to pass
Trying to race the bars
Of prison that hold me par

He came like a knight of light
Held me in his arms so tight
Called for my name again
And i made him my friend again

He was called my Gramary
That brought all my faith again

A KISS

Talked about the day
Had nothing else to say
Well we went to that quiet place
To have a kiss to replace

A kiss so strong it broke all chords
A kiss so long it came along
A kiss to miss all secrets gone
A kiss which said you're not alone

His lips now only craved for her taste
Her smile made him want it again
They kissed so sweet the flowers bloomed
She smelled like him and he liked the moon.

INVISIBLE LAYERS

Layers of air unheaven
Layers of smile unbeaten
Everyone have it as their own
Carry it like a newborn
Walk with it like none
Walk to it like one
Everyone has their own layer
Invisible as the air
They don't let others cross it
And if crossed that's all they care

You've got yours and I've got mine
Invisible layers of comfort and mime

OVER YOU

I'm Happy you've got some new friends
I've seen how hard you've been
I hope you get what you become
I think I'll be over you now

I met new friends and old
I cleansed all the dead souls
I feared facing alone
But i know I'm over you now

IT'S A FIGHT

It's a fight
It's not about who's wrong who's right
It's a fight
It's not about who danced who cried
It's a fight
Never been in so much trouble alive

They're not a knight
Just two people wanting different lives
They're not a knight
Just what they want they realized that night
They're not a knight
They're just two lovers who're not there anymore.

FROM ME TO YOU

Up across the room
There you are
Between all the faces
And after all the glass

Saw me to you
I want everybody to leave
From me to you
I hate everybody too much

Saw me walk to you
And have small talks
With all the unknown faces
And students from the same class

Walked me to you
I crossed everybody
To talk to you
I skipped everybody

Thank you guys for reading it and your attention towards my work is appreciated. It's been lovely to write and being able to share my work with good people.

I hope my work made you think about life and yourself. Colors of life just showcases the different phases of life and helps us appreciate the goodness in each.

All of us have our own bad days and good days. I write just to make your good day a little better and you bad day not being worse than it already is.

It was a pleasure being able to assist you in any way possible.

Thank you
Hansika Parmar